What's in Your Dabba?

Celebrities, Chefs and Foodies Share Their Favourite Easy Recipes

FROM THE
EDITORS OF TWEAK INDIA

FOOD CONSULTANT AND PHOTOGRAPHER
VERNIKA AWAL

tweakbooks   ❋ juggernaut

JUGGERNAUT BOOKS
C-I-128, First Floor, Sangam Vihar, Near Holi Chowk,
New Delhi 110 080, India

First published by Juggernaut Books 2020

10 9 8 7 6 5 4 3 2 1

P-ISBN: 9789353451233
E-ISBN: 9789353451240

Design by Tavishi Sahu
Typeset by R. Ajith Kumar

Printed and bound at Thomson Press India Ltd

Contents

Foreword

TWINKLE KHANNA

'What's in your dabba?' This question reverberates around playgrounds and office cafeterias across India – as pigtailed girls grab jalebis from airtight containers in exchange for pakoras from their own and my colleagues all eye the fried arbi in the accountant's clearly initialled steel box.

One would think that movie stars would be above dabba envy but my partner once returned from a shoot with a grievous complaint. I was sending him chauli and tendli, while his co-star, a long-standing bachelor, was unpacking lunch boxes filled with prawns and lobster.

'That's because it's not a wife but his mummy who sends across his lunch! Considering the poor woman has been sending him a dabba for the last forty-eight years, she has had a lot more practice than me,' I said flippantly, though I was feeling distinctly inadequate. It didn't help that this comment was made over dinner at my in-laws'.

Packing dabbas every morning is a quintessentially Indian phenomenon. If we were a nation of people who would just nip out to grab a sandwich for lunch, we would not be haunted by existential questions like how do we break the monotony of aloo parathas on alternate days? How many chutney sandwiches are acceptable before we are classified as indifferent mothers? Am I going to be judged forever by a tendli in a tiffin box?

Early this year, bogged down by planning weekly menus for the family, I began asking people what they were putting in their dabbas. Friends, colleagues and Tweak readers sent in recipes and I began trying them out. A sweet potato twist to the regular sabudana khichdi. A new spin that turned theplas into tacos.

The meals I was putting together became scrumptious. It wasn't just my younger one, even my weighing scale was grateful. Her purple unicorn container was now empty, so I had no leftovers to polish off on the way back from the school pick-up, in an absent-minded stupor.

Then the pandemic hit. And people brought out their pots and pans with a vengeance. Cooking, a necessity, now became an expression of joy, a way of reaching out for solace, a gentle escape.

Mothers and aunts were frantically called with questions of how long moong dal had to be soaked to make chillas or what to use if there was no asafoetida in the cupboard. Even my mother, who can barely boil an egg, entered the kitchen, armed with an apron and a borrowed recipe.

I teased her, rather publicly, saying, 'It only took forty-six years, a pandemic and an extended lockdown for my mother to make me my first meal, fried rice.' But she had no time for me as she was engrossed in her next project, learning how to make my sister-in-law's infamous rum cake. Meanwhile, I had friends asking me to give them the recipe for my mother's simple fried rice!

We could not share meals, so we shared recipes. Slices of our past and fresh explorations. Both topped with layers of improvisations, because we had to make do with what we had till the next grocery run.

There was hope in the form of a beetroot burger, which we knew we would once again pack into dabbas when schools and offices reopened. We found support in more experienced cooks when we shared stories of our small burns and not-quite-round chapattis. Failures in the form of a curdled tiramisu were swallowed along with our pride. Triumphs were gleefully gulped down, before we could take a picture for posterity.

The idea for this book, like the moong beans that I had soaked to sprinkle over my clumsily chopped salad, germinated slowly. It had begun its journey in the best of times and, in the spirit of Dickens's famous first line, it continued taking shape through the worst. Food as a way of connecting people remained unchanged, though the world itself was unrecognizable.

This is a cookbook for today when we eat alone and for tomorrow, when we will eat together. The way we used to, unmasked and undaunted. All our senses engaged. Our eyes darting from plates to faces. Our ears catching snippets of conversations and clanging cutlery. Our noses following criss-crossing aromas as we sit around with our opened dabbas, a mandala of dishes, across long tables.

The humble lunch box, holding centre stage in our little book, has inspired movies, started romances, cemented friendships. But above all it is representative of a singularly Indian notion – that takeaways and restaurants are occasional indulgences, but nothing beats our own ghar ka khana. Well, unless you are sent a dabba full of tendli, while someone else is sitting across the table chomping on butter garlic prawns.

Lunch dabba

A satisfying main meal that you can take with
you anywhere or eat at home.
Most of the dishes here are healthy,
easy to make and delicious.

Note: Most recipes are vegetarian
with non-vegetarian options included where suitable.
All recipes feed four, unless specified otherwise.

Jasleen Marwah's

Aloo Sliders with Walnut Chutney

 NUTS INCLUDED

Kashmiri flavours – asafoetida, mustard oil, fennel seeds and ginger powder – come together in a phenomenal slider by home chef Jasleen Marwah.

Ingredients

½ kg potatoes	2 tbsp curd
4 buns	¼ tsp ginger powder
4 tbsp mustard oil	2 tsp fennel seed powder
¼ tsp asafoetida	1 tsp salt
1 bay leaf	2 tbsp cornflour
2 cloves	2 tbsp roasted semolina
3 tsp Kashmiri red chilli powder	2 cups water
	Regular cooking oil

Preparation

Boil the potatoes and remove the skin once they cool down.

Mash the potatoes well with your hand, a fork or a potato masher.

Heat mustard oil in a pan. Bring it to smoking point and let it cool down.

Turn the gas back on and put asafoetida in the oil.

Add one bay leaf and two cloves.

Turn off the gas to prevent the masalas from burning.

Add Kashmiri red chilli powder.

Turn on the gas after two minutes. Add a bit of water to keep the chilli powder from burning.

Keep the gas on low flame and add the curd.

Keep stirring the mixture till the oil separates from the curd. At this point the oil should be bright red.

Once the oil separates, add a bit of water.

Now add ginger powder and fennel seed powder.

Add salt and mix well till there is no water left in the pan.

Now add the mashed potatoes to this mixture and mix thoroughly.

Meanwhile, make a slurry of cornflour.

Spread out some semolina on a plate to coat the aloo tikkis with.

Keep a non-stick pan and some regular cooking oil ready for shallow frying.

Once the potato mixture has cooled down, start making tikkis (remove the whole spices added earlier).

Heat the non-stick pan and put 2 tbsp of oil in it.

Dip the tikki in the slurry, gently coat it with the semolina and slide it into the pan.

Cook until both sides are nicely brown and crisp. The semolina will give a crispy crunch to the outside while the inside will remain soft like a dum aloo.

To assemble the slider, heat the bun in the OTG. Take it out once it is crisp, place the tikki inside it, and then add the walnut chutney, fresh mint leaves and roughly chopped walnuts.

Walnut chutney

½ cup walnuts, soaked for two hours

1 cup curd

½ cup mint leaves

2 green chillies, deseeded

Salt to taste

Preparation

While the walnuts are soaking in water, hang the curd in a muslin cloth to drain out excess water.

After two hours, blend the walnuts with the mint leaves and green chillies in a blender (you can keep the mixture slightly coarse). Then add the hung curd and salt. Add some chopped green chillies if you want a spicy punch in the chutney.

❝*A favourite in our family, it is like tasting flavours from the Kashmir Valley, but with a twist!*❞

Chinu Vaze's

Aubergine and Quinoa Salad with Tahini Dressing

⊘ **HIGH PROTEIN**

Celebrity chef Chinu Vaze's Middle East–inspired multicoloured salad, featuring a healthy quinoa base, aubergine caviar and a delicious apple cider tahini dressing, will open up a whole new world of flavours for you.

Ingredients

1 cup quinoa

3 cups water

1 tsp salt

3 tbsp olive oil

1½ tbsp lemon juice

½ tsp salt

Tahini dressing

3 tbsp tahini

4 tbsp orange juice

2 tbsp apple cider vinegar

½ tbsp agave nectar/maple syrup/ honey

¼ tsp salt

3 tbsp olive oil

Aubergine caviar

1 roasted aubergine (bharta style)

1 tsp olive oil

4 garlic cloves, roasted and chopped

¼ cup spring onions

2 tbsp yogurt

½ tsp lemon juice

½ tsp paprika

¼ tsp salt

½ cup pomegranate

3 tsp roasted and slivered almonds

8 cherry tomatoes

Preparation

Put quinoa, water and salt in a covered saucepan and cook for
15 minutes or till the water evaporates.

Keep it covered for another 10 minutes.

Transfer the quinoa into a tray and fluff with a fork. Add olive oil,
lemon juice and salt.

To roast the aubergine, rub it with olive oil and turn it over an open
flame for 12 minutes or till it softens.

Remove the peel and chop roughly. You should have around 1 cup of
roasted aubergine.

Add chopped garlic, chopped spring onions, yogurt, lemon juice,
paprika, pomegranate, cherry tomatoes and slivered almonds and
mix well.

To make the tahini dressing, mix tahini, orange juice, apple cider
vinegar, honey/maple syrup/agave nectar and salt.

Add a little olive oil as you whisk. It will be thinner than a regular
dressing. Mix this with the quinoa.

Put it in a bowl, add a spoonful of aubergine caviar and almond flakes
and serve.

*❝Tahini is one of my favourite condiments – it's luscious,
delicious and also really good for you. This dressing is definitely
one of my go-tos!❞*

Natasha Gandhi's

Millet Baati

⊛ HEALTHY GRAIN   ⊛ GLUTEN-FREE

Food entrepreneur Natasha Gandhi puts
on her chef's hat to update this traditional
recipe from the deserts of India.

Courtesy Natasha Gandhi

Ingredients

½ cup sorghum flour
½ cup amaranth flour
Boiling water
1 tbsp ghee
1 tsp salt
½ tsp baking powder

Preparation

In a bowl add all the dry ingredients and
ghee and mix well.

Add boiling water gradually and knead to
make a dough.

Preheat the oven for 10 minutes at 180 °C.

Shape the dough into lemon-sized balls and
grease them with ghee using a brush.

Bake in the preheated oven for 25 minutes
at 180 °C.

Brush with some ghee once they are out of
the oven.

Serve hot with dal and churma.

❝ *Traditionally, baati is made using whole wheat flour and loads of ghee.
This gluten-free version uses sorghum and amaranth, with just a little
ghee to knead the dough and brush the baati before serving.* ❞

Nmami Agarwal's

Beetroot Burgers

◉ KID-FRIENDLY

Deceptively dressed as the universally beloved 'pattice', nutritionist Nmami Agarwal's healthy beetroot and veggie tikkis are a con job that will win you the award for mother of the year. The perfect meal for kids when topped with a dollop of pink beetroot hummus and sandwiched between soft multigrain buns.

Ingredients

4 multigrain slider buns

1 medium-sized beetroot

¼ cup chopped carrots, beans and bell peppers

2 tsp beetroot hummus spread

2 tsp rolled oats

2 tsp sesame oil

Salt to taste

Pepper to taste

2 lettuce leaves

For the beetroot hummus

3 tbsp boiled chickpeas

¼ shredded beetroot

½ tsp tahini

Salt to taste

Preparation

For the beetroot hummus

Blend together boiled chickpeas, beetroot, tahini and salt. Keep the consistency thick and spreadable. Add water if needed. Keep aside.

For the burgers

Boil the beetroot and chopped veggies. Strain the water and keep aside. Allow the vegetables to cool and then cut into small pieces.

In a food processor, blend beets, vegetables, rolled oats, salt and pepper using the strained water. Make sure the paste is thick.

Shape the mixture into small patties.

Heat sesame oil in a shallow pan and fry the patties on both sides.

Arrange the buns on a flat surface, place the lettuce leaf inside and top it with the cooked patty. Spread a teaspoon of hummus over it.

Serve immediately or pack it in your kid's tiffin!

❝Give your regular, fat-loaded burgers a healthy twist with these mini beetroot burgers that taste great and are high on the nutritional value index. These will surely be relished by your little ones.❞

Ritu Dalmia's

Bhindi Salan

🥜 NUTS INCLUDED

Bhindi (okra) is the vegetable equivalent of that girl in school who got along with everyone and took part in all competitions. Celebrity chef Ritu Dalmia's bhindi salan is a hybrid tweak of the desi favourite.

Ingredients

300 g okra, slit
¼ cup tamarind pulp
2 tbsp oil
Salt to taste
½ tsp sugar
Juice of 1 lemon
1 tbsp chopped coriander
1 tsp crushed peanuts for garnish
Water

Spices for the tadka

½ tsp fenugreek seeds
½ tsp black mustard seeds
¼ tsp asafoetida

For the paste

1 medium-sized onion, chopped
2 garlic cloves
¼ cup toasted peanuts
2 medium-sized tomatoes, blanched
½-inch ginger
½ tsp cumin seeds
2–3 green chillies
2 tsp sesame seeds

Preparation

Blend all the ingredients for the paste in a food blender till smooth and keep aside.

In a heavy-bottomed pan, heat 2 tbsp oil.

Add fenugreek, mustard and asafoetida.

When the spices start to sputter, add the paste and cook on low flame till the oil starts floating on top.

Add tamarind paste, salt, lemon juice, sugar and some water and cook on low heat again.

In a separate pan, heat oil and fry the slit okra.

Mix the fried okra with the paste and cook for another few minutes.

Garnish with the peanuts, coriander and sesame seeds and serve with parathas or rice.

The lockdown was a strange time for me – I did not want to cook any Italian or European food. The only cooking that would comfort me was Indian home food. This recipe is a combination of two recipes: the khatti bhindi recipe given to me by my friend Arundhati Katju and the traditional salan recipe given by a friend from Hyderabad.

Namrata Shirodkar's

Bhindi Poriyal

This Tamil-style okra dish courtesy actor
Namrata Shirodkar will have you licking
your fingers. Featuring a range of flavours –
pungent mustard, earthy cumin and fresh
coconut – green veggies have never looked
better. Best paired with roti or rice.

Ingredients

1¼ cup bhindi (okra)

1 tsp oil

½ tsp mustard seeds

½ tsp cumin seeds

8–10 curry leaves

¼ cup chopped onion

1 green chilli, chopped

¼ cup freshly grated
coconut

A pinch of asafoetida

1 tsp turmeric powder

1 tbsp chopped coriander
leaves

Salt to taste

Preparation

Wash the okra twice and wipe with tissue or
a dry cloth.

Cut in circles and keep aside.

Heat some oil in a pan.

Add mustard seeds and cumin seeds.

Add asafoetida, turmeric, chopped onions
and curry leaves.

Add the coconut and okra and sauté.

Cook on low flame.

Add salt to taste.

Garnish with coriander.

❝This dish is a favourite because it satisfies my kids' Indian food
cravings. I like to keep it simple when it comes to what I feed them.
A healthy and wholesome meal with small indulgences.❞

Susan Millan's

Breast Bone Pepper Water

This wholesome mutton gravy dish by home chef Susan Millan is a spicier version of Mulligatawny soup. Warm and coconutty with rasam-like consistency, it is best enjoyed on a cold rainy day.

Ingredients

1 kg mutton (½ kg to ¾ kg breast bone + mutton meat)

½ tbsp oil

½ cup coconut milk

Juice of 2 lemons

8–10 curry leaves

Salt to taste

Coriander for garnish

For the masala, grind

2 onions

1-inch ginger

½ tsp turmeric

1 tsp cumin

2 green chillies

6–8 garlic cloves

Preparation

Heat oil in a pressure cooker on medium flame and put in the curry leaves.

Add the ground masala and cook till the raw onion smell goes away. You can add a little water if it gets too dry.

Then add the cleaned and washed mutton and fry for a few minutes on high flame.

Add salt to taste.

Add enough water to fully cover the mutton.

Pressure cook on high flame and after one whistle, turn the gas on low and let it cook for 10 minutes.

Once the cooker has cooled, open and check the mutton. It should be cooked but if you feel it is not, put it on for another whistle.

When you open the cooker again, check the consistency of the gravy. It should not be thick like a curry but thin like rasam.

Add coconut milk and mix. Stir in the lime juice.

Garnish with fresh coriander and serve with hot rice.

Anglo-Indians have the funniest names for their tastiest dishes. All my life I have loved my family's version of Breast Pepper Water, only to find out recently that the said dish is actually called Breast Bone Pepper Water.

Bhumi Pednekar's

Chicken Curry

The actor's favourite creamy, spicy chicken
gravy feels like home.

Ingredients

For the chicken marinade

3 cups boneless chicken
½ cup curd
1 tbsp grated garlic
1 tbsp grated ginger
2 tsp garam masala
1 tsp cumin powder
1 tsp coriander powder
1 tsp red chilli powder
1 tsp salt

For the gravy

1 bay leaf
1 black cardamom
*1 medium-sized onion, finely
chopped*
4–5 garlic cloves
*3 medium-sized tomatoes, finely
chopped*
5–6 cashews
1 tsp garam masala
1 tsp cumin powder
1 tsp coriander powder
1 tsp red chilli powder
Salt to taste
5 tbsp oil

Preparation

In a bowl, combine the chicken with all the ingredients for
the marinade and massage it for 5 minutes. Leave it to rest for
30–40 minutes.

Heat 2 tbsp oil in a pan on medium flame.

Add the chicken pieces to it in batches of two or three (make sure not to crowd the pan).

Pan-fry these pieces for 2–3 minutes on each side till they turn golden brown.

Keep aside once done.

To make the gravy, heat 3 tbsp oil in a pan.

Add the bay leaf, black cardamom and cumin.

Once they begin to crackle, add the onion and garlic and cook till they turn golden.

Add the tomatoes and cashews and cook till the tomatoes soften.

Switch off the gas and let the mix cool.

Make a paste of it in a mixer grinder.

In a pan, cook the paste, garam masala, coriander powder, chilli powder and salt to taste.

Let it cook till the rawness goes away and the mixture starts separating from the oil.

Add the chicken pieces to it.

Garnish with finely chopped coriander and serve.

❝Eat well and right, then there's no fight. In my dabba I have chicken curry, stir-fried mushrooms, isabgol tikki and almond flour roti. Like Ma says, 'Be generous.'❞

Dimple Kapadia's

Bhutta Curry

The actor's favourite bhutta curry drenches corn cobs in a wholesome flavourful gravy with a ghee, curry leaf and mustard tadka, garnished with a handful of fresh coriander. Best paired with roti or rice. You can also make this dish with chicken or mutton kofta.

Ingredients

3 corn cobs, cut into three pieces each

1 coconut, cut into small pieces

2–3 green chillies

5–6 garlic cloves

A handful of fresh coriander

Salt to taste

1¼ cups curd

½ cup coconut milk

1 tbsp ghee

5–6 curry leaves

1 tsp mustard

Preparation

For the masala, grind coconut pieces along with garlic, chillies and fresh coriander.

In a pan, mix coconut milk and ground masala and stir well.

Then add the curd and continue stirring.

Put the pan on the stove and keep stirring till the mix becomes a little thick, and then add the corn cobs and salt.

Once the corn cobs are cooked, give them a tadka of ghee, curry leaves and mustard.

Garnish with the coriander.

❝No celebration in the family is really complete unless we have bhutta curry on the table — my mum's recipe is the one we've grown up eating. ❞

Shaheen Abbas's

Chilli Chicken

Jewellery designer Shaheen Abbas has cracked the code for restaurant-worthy chilli chicken with her signature recipe – boneless chicken marinated in a ginger–garlic heavy paste, sautéed with a mix of sauces and vegetables. Best paired with rice.

Ingredients

2 cups cubed boneless chicken

2 tbsp finely chopped ginger

2 tbsp finely chopped garlic

2 onions, diced

1 capsicum, diced

3 green chillies, halved and slit

1–2 stalks spring onion, chopped

¼ cup all-purpose flour

1 tbsp ginger–garlic paste

½ tsp crushed peppercorns

2 tbsp dark soy sauce

1 tbsp red chilli sauce

½ tsp honey

Salt to taste

Sesame oil

2 tbsp cornflour powder

Water

Directions for marinating and frying

In a bowl, add chicken cubes, salt, crushed peppercorns and ginger–garlic paste and mix well.

Take all-purpose flour in another bowl. Add cornflour and some water and whisk well to make a semi-thick slurry.

Dip marinated chicken cubes in the slurry, slide into hot oil and deep-fry till golden and crisp.

Drain on absorbent paper.

Preparation

Heat the sesame oil in a wok.

Add the garlic and ginger and fry till they turn golden.

Add the onions, capsicum, green chillies and spring onion.

Fry on high flame.

Add dark soy sauce and red chilli sauce and honey.

Add chicken cubes.

Add cornflour dissolved in water.

Let this cook for 2–3 minutes on high flame.

Garnish with finely chopped spring onion and serve.

It's like a comforting, familiar hug, but in a bowl.

Amninder Sandhu's

Tandoori Chicken with Broccoli

Looking for the perfect high-protein, low-carb lunch? Look no further than chef Amninder Sandhu's delicious roasted chicken with a healthy side of broccoli.

Ingredients

For the tandoori chicken

*4 whole chicken legs
(drumsticks and thighs,
skinless)*

3 tbsp mustard oil

1 tsp coriander powder

1 tsp cumin powder

1 tsp turmeric powder

1 tsp red chilli powder

1 cup curd

1 tbsp lemon juice

4 garlic cloves, crushed

2 tbsp minced fresh ginger

Salt to taste

For the broccoli

1 broccoli

Salt to taste

Pepper to taste

Preparation

For the tandoori chicken

Heat the mustard oil in a small pan over medium heat.

Remove from heat and add all the masalas/spices.

Whisk this into the curd along with lemon juice, garlic, ginger and salt.

Make deep slashes in the chicken and coat with the marinade.

Refrigerate for 6–8 hours. Keep overnight for best results.

Preheat the oven to 220 °C. Remove the excess marinade and cook the chicken for about half an hour, basting with butter every now and then, till it begins to brown.

Serve hot.

For the broccoli

Cut the broccoli into florets.

Sauté in butter and season with salt and pepper.

" *Tandoori chicken is the ultimate comfort food for me. I have grown up eating it, and it just makes everyone happy.* **"**

Indu Arora's

Stuffed Chillas

⊛ HIGH PROTEIN   ⊘ KID-FRIENDLY

Home chef Indu Arora's healthy moong
dal chilla is the perfect hiding place for
all the veggies you don't want your kids
to know they're eating – from carrots and
capsicum to onions. Grated paneer and
crunchy pomegranate add just the right
amount of texture to keep things exciting.

Ingredients

1 cup moong dal

¼-inch ginger

1 green chilli

¼ cup water

Salt to taste

For the filling

½ cup grated paneer

*Pomegranate seeds from half a
pomegranate*

¼ tsp chaat masala

2 tbsp grated carrot

2 tbsp finely chopped onion

2 tbsp finely chopped capsicum

Salt to taste

Preparation

Soak the moong dal in water.

Blend the dal with the ginger, green chillies, water and salt to form a
runny paste.

Heat a non-stick pan and spread one large ladle of batter and cook on
both sides.

In a separate bowl, mix the paneer, pomegranate seeds, carrot, onion
and capsicum and chaat masala.

Spoon some mixture on to the cooked chilla and roll.

Serve with green chutney, ketchup or any other sauce of your choice.

* ¼ cup moong dal will make two small chillas and needs only 10 minutes of soaking.

"This is ideal for all those moms whose children scrunch up their noses at the sight of dal, roti and sabzi. Sneak in the dal by mixing it in the chilla batter, add the veggies of your choice in the stuffing, and present it beautifully. It really does work; I still sneak in all sorts of vegetables in my daughter's food without her suspecting a thing, and she is twenty-five now!"

Anushruti RK's

Spicy Chilli

A nutritious one-pot meal that packs in a boatload of vegetables and a fiery punch, food blogger Anushruti RK's Indian take on Texan chilli is best paired with steamed rice or bread. You can also make this dish with keema.

Ingredients

¼ cup kidney beans

3 tbsp oil

2 green chillies (deseeded if you can't handle the heat!)

½ tsp asafoetida

2–3 sticks of celery, cut into tiny pieces

1 green bell pepper, diced

1 red bell pepper, diced

2 cups pureed tomatoes

1 tsp brown sugar

½ cup cooked corn

1 tsp cumin powder

Freshly ground black pepper to taste

¾ tsp red chilli powder or to taste

2 tsp dried parsley or 2 tbsp fresh parsley, chopped

1 tsp dried oregano

½ tsp thyme

2 tsp salt or to taste

1 cup crumbled fresh cheese

Preparation

Soak the kidney beans overnight or for a minimum of 6 hours. Drain and cook the kidney beans with 2½ cups of water in a pressure cooker. Alternatively, you can use a saucepan. Reserve the water.

In a saucepan or a wok, heat the oil. Put in the chillies, asafoetida and celery sticks and stir-fry for a few seconds. Add the chopped bell peppers and cook for a few minutes until the pepper turns soft.

Put in pureed tomatoes and cook for 4–5 minutes or till the oil separates. Stir in the sugar to balance the tart flavour of the tomatoes. Add the corn, all the spices and the rest of the ingredients. Cook until the tomato is dry.

Stir in the kidney beans along with the reserved water and let it simmer for 15–20 minutes.

Stir in the paneer, mix well and cook for a couple more minutes. Serve hot or at room temperature with plain steamed rice or breads of your choice.

❝*The chilli is enriched with many complex yet subtle flavours. Kidney beans and crumbled fresh cheese ensure that it is also bursting with protein.* ❞

Raina Kshetry's

Kolkata Egg Roll

What the vada pav is to Mumbai and the tikki is to Delhi, the paratha roll is to Kolkata. Food blogger Raina Kshetry's recipe really hits the spot if you're missing the City of Joy.

Ingredients

To make two rolls

2 eggs

1 onion, chopped

1 tbsp milk

2 small green chillies (or as per preference)

2 lime wedges

½ tsp honey

Salt to taste

½ tsp pepper

Tomato sauce and green chilli sauce (as per taste)

Oil

Ready-made wheat/Malabar/ home-made parathas if you want it on the go and ready in 10 minutes. You can also make the paratha from scratch.

To make the paratha

2 cups all-purpose flour

2 tbsp oil (or ghee, as preferred)

½ tsp salt

A pinch of sugar (optional)

1 tsp baking powder (optional)

Cold water to knead the dough

Preparation

Beat the eggs with salt, pepper and honey till fluffy.

Heat 1 tsp oil in a large frying pan or tawa and put the beaten eggs. Make sure the egg mixture covers the base of the pan.

Keep the heat at medium low as eggs cook quickly and honey tends to stick to the pan on high flame.

Once the egg mixture is semi-raw in texture, place the paratha over it, pressing it gently with the help of a spatula. This will ensure the paratha sticks to the egg mixture.

Apply oil or ghee on the paratha and let it cook for 2–3 minutes.

Flip it over and fry the other side till the desired crispness is achieved and brown spots begin to appear.

To assemble the roll

Place the egg paratha on butter paper or a kitchen tissue.

Top it with green chillies, sliced onions and a generous squeeze of lime.

Sprinkle salt and pepper if you like, as well as a dash of tomato sauce or green chilli sauce.

Wrap the roll in the butter paper and tuck in at one end to seal neatly.

Serve immediately.

I'm quintessentially a Kolkata girl despite being born a Punjabi, and rolls have been really close to my heart. So I stepped into the kitchen and conjured up my own rendition of the all-time classic Kolkata egg roll.

Katrina Kaif's

Idli and Coconut Chutney

🌾 HEALTHY GRAIN   🌾 GLUTEN-FREE

🍩 BREAKFAST

We finally have something in common with Katrina Kaif.
We love soft, fluffy idlis as much as she does. This rice- and dal-
based dish paired with coconut chutney is the original happy
meal, perfect for your kid's and your own lunch.

Ingredients

For the idli

4 cups parboiled rice
¾ cup split urad dal
Water
Salt to taste

For the chutney

*1 cup freshly grated
coconut*
*2 tbsp roasted chana dal
or peanuts*
2 green chillies
½ cup water
Salt to taste

For tempering

1 tsp oil
½ tsp mustard seeds
½ tsp urad dal
1 sprig curry leaves

Preparation

For the idli batter

Wash the rice and soak for 2–4 hours.

Wash the urad dal and soak in a separate vessel for 3 hours.

Drain the excess water and grind the urad dal in a mixer grinder until
the batter turns fluffy and light. Transfer to a large bowl.

Drain the excess water from the soaked rice and grind to a smooth consistency.

Mix the rice batter with the urad dal batter and salt.

Beat the batter to make it airy and allow it to ferment in a warm place for 6–8 hours.

For the idli steamer

Grease the idli plates with some oil.

Spoon the batter into the plates.

Steam cook till done.

Remove the plates from the steamer.

Let the plates cool for 5–7 minutes and use a spoon to take out the idlis and serve.

For the coconut chutney

Put the coconut, chana dal and green chillies in the mixer grinder.

Add water and allow it to soak for around 5 minutes.

Grind it coarsely.

Transfer it to a serving bowl.

Heat oil in a small pan/iron ladle and temper with mustard seeds, urad dal and curry leaves.

Pour over the chutney.

Mix well and serve with idlis.

"I try to keep my food simple and have been taught by my nutritionist not to be afraid of eating rice, so here's my favourite rice idli and chutney."

Pernia Qureshi's

Scrambled Eggs

⊙ **BREAKFAST**   ⊙ **HIGH PROTEIN**

We love scrambled eggs as much as fashion entrepreneur Pernia Qureshi does. It may seem simple, but this protein-heavy snack is eggsactly what amateur cooks struggle with. This three-ingredient recipe will ensure you avoid the 'too runny' or 'too gluggy' curse.

Ingredients

4 eggs
¼ cup milk
2 tsp butter
A pinch of black pepper
Salt to taste

Preparation

Beat eggs, milk, salt and pepper in a bowl until blended.

Heat butter in a large non-stick skillet over medium heat until hot.

Pour in egg mixture and keep stirring.

Continue cooking till it is thick and no visible liquid egg remains.

Remove from heat.

Serve immediately with freshly toasted bread.

❝*I have always struggled with portion control and a sugar addiction. But I have realized that if you consume nutritious food then you don't end up eating as much.* ❞

Twinkle Khanna's

Ragi and Rava Idlis

Courtesy Twinkle Khanna

🌾 **HEALTHY GRAIN**　　🍴 **KID-FRIENDLY**

Twinkle Khanna makes these nutritious ragi idlis for her kids, but if we're being honest, these are too good for adults to resist.

Ingredients

1 cup rava

1 cup ragi flour

Salt to taste

1 cup curd

1 cup water, add as required

¼ tsp baking soda/ cooking soda

Preparation

Dry roast the rava on medium flame for 2–3 minutes. Cool it down completely.

Transfer it to a large mixing bowl.

Add ragi flour, salt, curd and water as required.

Mix well and keep aside for 30 minutes.

Mix again and add water if required.

Before steaming, add a pinch of baking soda and mix till frothy.

Brush the idli mould with oil and immediately pour the batter into it.

Steam for 8–10 minutes on medium flame.

Rest for 5–10 minutes before unmoulding.

Serve hot with coconut chutney and sambar.

❝*I may not always be around to watch what my kids are eating, so here are some healthy treats that I put inside their dabbas.* ❞

Nikhil Merchant's

Coffee Barbeque Jackfruit Sliders

Jackfruit sliders are here to stir vegetarians out of the aloo–paneer–veggie trifecta that has haunted their burger dreams since we traded pavs for buns. Food consultant Nikhil Merchant's jackfruit stuffing slathered with a coffee barbecue (BBQ) sauce and ensconced in soft buns is a party in the mouth. You can also make this recipe using pulled pork or shredded chicken.

Ingredients

For the jackfruit stuffing

4 cups raw (green) jackfruit chunks, skinned and seeded

2 tsp smoked paprika powder

1 tsp cumin powder

3 tsp brown sugar

Salt to taste

White pepper to taste

2 tbsp oil

1½ cups coffee BBQ sauce

Sides and to serve

12 slider buns
Coleslaw
Grated cheddar cheese
Ground mustard sauce
Arugula leaves
Coffee BBQ sauce

For the coffee BBQ sauce

12 large tomatoes, seeded and chunked

2 tbsp neutral oil

1 large red onion, sliced

6 garlic cloves, crushed

½ cup brewed coffee (try not to use the instant one, espresso works best)

1 cup brown sugar

4 dried Kashmiri red chillies, soaked in ½ cup hot water

2 tbsp smoked paprika

1 cup balsamic vinegar

3 bay leaves

200 g concentrated tomato paste

Salt to taste

Preparation

For the coffee BBQ sauce

Before starting on the coffee BBQ sauce, dry the jackfruit chunks in a colander covered with paper towels.

Heat oil in a large saucepot/Dutch oven and stir-fry the onion and garlic till they release their aromas.

Stir in the tomato paste and cook till it starts browning slightly and all the water has dried up.

Add the coffee, stir for 2 minutes and then add the rest of the ingredients.

Simmer for a little over an hour on low heat, stirring occasionally, till you have a sludgy mix of melted fruit.

Remove the bay leaves, transfer the mix to a blender and puree to a smooth paste.

Strain through a fine strainer, cool and store/use (this can be used for a month if refrigerated).

For the jackfruit stuffing

Sprinkle dry spice powders on the jackfruit.

Heat oil in a large pan and add the jackfruit chunks. Stir on high heat till the fruit starts browning on the edges.

Add a cup of the coffee BBQ sauce along with ¼ cup water. Cover and cook for about 15 minutes on medium heat.

Open the lid and tear apart the cooked jackfruit chunks with two forks, revealing a meaty, stringy textured fruit (pulled style). Dry up the sauce a bit on the gas if it is not already.

To assemble the sliders

Split and butter the slider buns, slather with mustard sauce on one side and coffee BBQ sauce on the other.

Layer with arugula, coleslaw and the pulled jackfruit stuffing and sprinkle cheese on top. Serve warm.

This recipe is sure to win the hearts of your guests and family alike! A vegetarian's perfect answer to pulled meat dishes.

Prerna Gupta's

Vegetable Paniyarams

🌾 GLUTEN-FREE   ✐ KID-FRIENDLY

Made from leftover idli batter, crispy on the outside and soft inside, food blogger Prerna Gupta's veggie-stuffed paniyarams will dupe your kids into eating veggies. Because if they can't see them, they're not there. Best paired with tangy tomato chutney.

Ingredients

3 cups leftover idli/dosa batter

1 onion, finely chopped

½ tsp finely chopped/grated ginger

1 medium-sized carrot, grated

1 capsicum, finely chopped

1 green chilli, chopped (optional if making for kids)

½ tsp turmeric powder

¼ tsp red chilli powder (optional)

Salt to taste

1 tbsp oil

½ tsp mustard seeds

1 tsp urad dal

5–6 curry leaves

⅓ tsp asafoetida

1 tbsp finely chopped coriander leaves

Preparation

Wash the dal and keep aside for 10 minutes.

Heat 1 tbsp oil in a non-stick pan and add the mustard seeds. When they sputter, add the asafoetida and dal.

When the dal turns a little golden, add the ginger, green chillies and curry leaves. Sauté for 10–20 seconds.

Add the onions and sauté for another 30 seconds.

Add the carrots and green pepper. Sauté till the onions are pink and the vegetables are cooked.

Add salt, turmeric powder and red chilli powder.

Add chopped coriander leaves.

Let the mixture cool and then add it to the idli batter and mix.

Grease a paniyaram pan with a few drops of oil and heat it for a minute before pouring in the batter.

Cook covered for 2–3 minutes on medium to low flame.

Flip with the help of a skewer/toothpick and cook until golden on both sides.

Serve hot with onion–tomato chutney or coriander chutney.

❝My eight-year-old eats all vegetables. My three-year-old, on the other hand, hates them. So we made these appams and my elder one told the three-year-old that they were alien ships and we needed to finish these to save ourselves. My little one didn't even notice the vegetables!**❞**

Gauri Devidayal's

Udon Noodles Stir-Fry with Salmon

You don't need to be a MasterChef contestant to ace home-style Japanese food, believes Gauri Devidayal, owner of The Table, one of Mumbai's top restaurants. These noodles may take longer than two minutes, but they're well worth the wait.

Ingredients

1 cup chopped broccoli

1 cup chopped mushrooms

4 garlic cloves, finely chopped

A handful of chopped coriander

1 tbsp soy sauce

1 tbsp oyster sauce

1 tbsp chilli oil (depending on your spice threshold)

100 g salmon

1 egg

2 tbsp olive oil

Salt to taste

1 packet of Udon noodles

Preparation

Boil water in a saucepan and add the Udon noodles.
Cook till the noodles are 90 per cent done.

In a separate pan, add a dash of olive oil and lightly pan-fry the salmon for 1 minute on each side.

Keep aside. Cut into thin slices after a few minutes.

Heat a pan and put 1 tbsp of olive oil.

Add the chopped garlic and cook till it turns golden brown.

Add a third of the chopped coriander and the broccoli florets.

After a few minutes, add the chopped mushrooms.

Add the oyster sauce, soy sauce and sweet chilli sauce as per taste.

Let it cook and then add the noodles and finally the salmon slices.

Optional: crack an egg in another pan and stir like you would to make scrambled eggs so that it's in small shreds. Add to the bowl of noodles.

"*I don't cook often, but when I do, I prefer this recipe because it's quick, yum and healthy. And I'm really happy that my daughter Dia has moved on from pesto pasta!*"

Kelvin Cheung's

Not-So-Authentic Street-Style Thai Flat Noodles

If you're craving noodles but can't handle the guilt of overindulging, grab a bowl of celebrity chef Kelvin Cheung's gluten-free noodles drenched in dark soy sauce, oyster sauce and flavourful coconut aminos, with egg for a little protein punch.

Ingredients

1 cup fresh wide, flat rice noodles, soaked overnight

1 onion, julienned

2 garlic cloves, sliced

3 scallions cut into sticks

1 cup curry leaves

1 egg

2 tbsp gluten-free sweet dark soy sauce

2 tbsp gluten-free oyster sauce

4 tbsp coconut aminos

Preparation

Prepare your rice noodles by soaking them in cold water for a few hours or overnight. Use your fingers to separate each noodle if they are stuck together.

Put oil in a wok and place it on high heat. Sear noodles until they get a slight crispy texture and season with 2 tbsp coconut aminos.

Set noodles aside.

Add the onions, spring onions and curry leaves and sauté until all the vegetables are cooked.

Push the vegetables to the side, forming a ring around the rim. Put more oil, and once hot, crack an egg into the wok.

Scramble the egg while the vegetables are still cooking on the rim.

Push the egg to the side and put the rice noodles back into the wok.

Season with dark soy sauce and oyster sauce.

Mix everything together and stir-fry until the sauce is fully absorbed and begins to caramelize.

Taste to check seasoning and serve immediately with a wedge of lime, lemon and your favourite hot sauce.

"*Like most children, my one-year-old son Bodhi loves noodles. Unlike most children, he dislikes the traditional mac 'n' cheese and pasta, preferring flat rice noodles instead. This dish is a family favourite and is on our menu every single week as it's easy to make and delicious.*"

Suman Agarwal's

Soya Keema Pav

🏃 **HIGH PROTEIN**

The cheat dish of our dreams, masala pav, gets a healthy 'pav'ered lift from nutritionist Suman Agarwal – her soya keema pav features soya granules dunked in a flavourful mix of veggies and sauces, paired with soft pav. You can also make this dish with chicken or mutton keema.

Ingredients

For the soya keema

1 cup soya granules

2 medium-sized onions, finely chopped

2 medium-sized tomatoes, finely chopped

½ cup finely chopped capsicum

½ cup grated cauliflower

2 tbsp finely chopped coriander

1 tbsp hot and sweet tomato chilli sauce

1 tbsp ginger, garlic and green chilli paste

½ tsp cumin powder

1 tsp pav bhaji masala

½ tsp chaat masala

½ tsp red chilli powder

Salt to taste

1 tsp oil

For the masala pav

6 pav

1 medium-sized onion, finely chopped

1 small tomato, finely chopped

2 tbsp finely chopped coriander

1 tsp pav bhaji masala

Salt to taste

1 tsp butter

Preparation

In a pan, cook soya granules in 3 cups of water on medium heat for 2–3 minutes. When the water starts frothing, turn off the flame.

Drain the granules in a colander and place under running water for a few seconds.

Squeeze out all the water from the granules and leave in the colander to dry.

Heat oil in a non-stick skillet and add ginger, garlic and green chilli paste.

Add onions and sauté until translucent.

Add capsicum and cook for a minute.

Add cauliflower and cook for a minute.

Add tomatoes and salt. Cover and cook for 2 minutes.

Add soya granules and ¼ cup water. Cover with a lid and cook for 5 minutes.

Remove the lid and add red chilli powder, turmeric powder, pav bhaji masala, chaat masala, cumin powder and ½ cup of water. Cook for 2 minutes.

Add hot and sweet sauce.

Garnish with fresh coriander.

Scoop out some bread from the top and bottom halves of each pav.

Fill ½ cup of the soya keema between each pav and keep aside.

Heat butter in a non-stick skillet.

Sauté onions until translucent.

Add tomatoes, pav bhaji masala, fresh coriander and salt.

Sauté for a minute and keep the mix aside.

On the same skillet, lightly roast the keema-filled pavs.

Garnish with the mix and serve.

I've always loved street food, be it in Kolkata or Mumbai. The soya keema pav is the perfect blend of the delicious flavour of street food and all the nutrients of a balanced meal!

Roshni Bajaj Sanghvi's

Spinach and Egg Dosa Pizza

 HIGH PROTEIN   KID-FRIENDLY

The dosa meets its match in a fibre-laden,
protein-filled spinach–egg mixture,
transforming into a dosa pizza – a healthy
meal by journalist and food writer Roshni Bajaj Sanghvi
that everyone from kids to tired mommies will enjoy.

Ingredients

¼ cup store-bought or home-made dosa batter

½ cup finely chopped spinach, blanched and tightly packed

1 whole egg, beaten

1 tsp garlic paste

¼ cup semi-firm cheese

½ tsp freshly cracked pepper

Salt to taste

2 tsp oil

Preparation

Brush an 8-inch seasoned skillet with oil and place it on the highest
flame of the small burner until the oil is hot.

Take the skillet off the heat, pour a ladleful of dosa batter in the
centre and tip and swirl the pan (as you would for a crêpe), until the
bottom of the skillet is coated with the batter. Make sure the batter is
spread evenly.

This dosa base needs to be a little thicker than the standard dosa, so
that it's sturdy enough to support the toppings without falling apart.

Put the skillet back on the heat. Once bubbles appear on the surface with the edges becoming translucent, lower the flame to minimum. Leave undisturbed until the batter is cooked through; the edges of the dosa will begin pulling away from the sides slightly and the bottom will be golden brown.

Flip the dosa and let the other side crisp to a light golden on low flame.

While the dosa is cooking, in a medium-sized bowl mix the spinach, beaten egg, garlic paste and pepper.

Flip the dosa again and pour half the spinach–egg mixture on to it and season with salt.

Cover the skillet for about 4–5 minutes and let the spinach–egg mixture set until there is no liquid from the egg or spinach left on the surface.

Grate an even layer of cheese all over the spinach–egg mixture. Cover again for about 2–3 minutes till the cheese melts.

Slide the pizza on to a flat plate or board, slice and serve hot, or refrigerate to reheat on a pan later.

Repeat with the other half of the dosa batter, spinach–egg mix and cheese to make two dosa pizzas.

❝*We're a pizza- and dosa-loving family. This mash-up recipe is a healthy hack loaded with veggies and proteins.*❞

Manasi Joshi Roy's

Pesto Pasta

A jar of pesto in the fridge can set you off on all kinds of cooking adventures. Add it to a cheese toastie, slather it over grilled fish or just eat it the way the Italians do using this recipe from actor Manasi Joshi Roy.

Ingredients

2 cups fresh basil

½ cup parmesan cheese

½ cup extra virgin olive oil

⅓ cup pine nuts/ cashews

3 garlic cloves

Salt to taste

Freshly ground pepper to taste

1 cup penne pasta

2 cups water

Preparation

Put all the ingredients for the pesto sauce together in a mixer grinder and make a coarse sauce out of it.

Cook the pasta in boiling hot water with salt to taste till it is al dente.

Once it is done, run the pasta under cold water and keep aside.

In a pan, add 1 tbsp olive oil, followed by the fresh pesto sauce.

Add the boiled pasta to it and toss it all together.

Garnish with parmesan cheese and serve.

❝*This pesto recipe is something I've been making ever since my daughter was six years old. She just turned eighteen, and it's still a hit with her. I always have this sauce in the fridge.* ❞

Kajal Mehta's

Protein Thepla Pizza

(icon) HIGH PROTEIN (icon) HEALTHY GRAIN

The founder of Kajal's Healthy Kitchen
believes in eating clean. Her dish is
a thepla base layered with overnight
nurture raita and served with vegetable salsa.

Ingredients

½ cup sorghum flour

½ cup porridge flour (ground oats)

½ cup millet flour

1 medium-sized sweet potato, boiled and mashed

½ cup finely chopped spinach

½ cup finely grated broccoli

Paste of 2 green chillies

A handful of coriander leaves

1 tsp coriander powder

1 tsp turmeric powder

1 avocado, mashed

1 tsp cumin seeds

A handful of chia seeds or any other seeds of your choice

Salt to taste

Preparation

In a large bowl, mix all the flours first, followed by all the dry ingredients and then add the vegetables.

Bind all the ingredients and make a fine dough that is easy to roll.

Now make even-sized balls from the dough and roll them out into thick circles as you would for chapattis.

Heat a pan and cook the rolled-out thepla on it.

When one side is done, flip it over and spread some oil on the half-cooked thepla.

Flip it again when the second side is cooked and spread some oil if required. Cook until it is golden brown.

Serve the healthy thepla with nurture raita, curry, pickles or just tea.

Overnight Nurture Raita

Ingredients

2 cups whole oats

2 cups coconut yogurt

1 carrot, grated

2 tbsp cranberry or any other dry berries

½ apple, chopped into small cubes

2 tbsp lemon juice

Himalayan salt to taste

¼ tsp red chilli powder

1 tbsp chia seeds

½ tsp cumin seed powder

1 tbsp desiccated coconut

1 tbsp chopped mint

Preparation

In a bowl, mix all the ingredients.

Pour the mixture into two small glasses or jars and leave it in the fridge overnight or for 3 hours to set.

Sprinkle some chopped mint on top and serve with protein bread or protein thepla.

Vegetable Salsa

Ingredients

½ carrot, grated
½ cucumber, grated
¼ beetroot, grated
1 small tomato, finely chopped
Juice of ½ lime
Himalayan salt to taste
Black pepper to taste

Preparation

In a bowl, mix all the ingredients.

To assemble the pizza

Spread the nurture raita on the protein thepla. Top it with the vegetable salsa and a sprinkle of pumpkin or sunflower seeds.

❝My take on healthy pizza comes from my love for my food heritage. One of the things I try to do is retain the flavours of that tradition but give it a slight modern twist and make it more nourishing.❞

Vicky Ratnani's

Urban Porridge

(✿) **HEALTHY GRAIN**

Dig deep into India's buffet of delicious millet varieties with chef Vicky Ratnani's delightfully earthy porridge.

Courtesy Vicky Ratnani

Ingredients

¼ cup kodo millet

2 tbsp sama rice

2 tbsp tuvar dal

¼ cup chickpeas

¼ cup moth beans/matki

3½ cups water

1 tbsp olive oil

1½ tsp ginger, garlic and green chilli paste

½ tsp asafoetida

1 tsp cumin seeds

2 Byadgi chillies, dried

15 curry leaves

½ cup chopped onions

1 cup chopped tomatoes

½ cup green peas

2 tsp coriander powder

1 tsp red chilli powder

½ tsp fennel seed powder

½ tsp garam masala

Juice of ½ lemon

1 tbsp chopped coriander leaves

Preparation

Wash and soak the kodo millet, chickpeas, tuvar dal and moth beans for at least 10 hours in 3½ cups of water.

Soak the sama rice for at least 30 minutes.

Heat the olive oil in a pan and sprinkle in the cumin seeds, Byadgi chillies, curry leaves and asafoetida.

Fry for 40 seconds.

Add the onions and ginger, garlic and green chilli paste and sauté.

Drain the millet and lentils and reserve the water.

Add the drained lentils to the drained sama rice and mix well.

Add the tomatoes and green peas and sauté for 4 minutes.

Add coriander powder, red chilli powder, fennel seed powder, garam masala, salt, white pepper and the reserved boiled liquid. Stir well.

Pressure cook for 3–5 whistles.

Garnish with fresh coriander leaves. Serve with raita and a crisp salad of your choice.

A healthy and nutritious one-pot meal that is loved by everyone in my family and friend circle.

Swati Iyer's

Spaghetti Aglio Olio

For those rushed days when you're juggling too many tasks, try entrepreneur Swati Iyer's version of the classic Italian meal, spiked with lemon and mushrooms. You can also add prawns to this dish.

Ingredients

100 g spaghetti

10–12 garlic cloves, chopped

4 tbsp olive oil

1 tsp red chilli flakes

Juice of 1 lemon

½ cup mushroom

1 tbsp chopped fresh basil

1 tsp fresh parsley

Lemon rind for aroma

Preparation

Put the spaghetti in boiling hot water with salt and a few drops of olive oil.

Cook till it is al dente. Drain and keep aside. Reserve some of the water.

Heat olive oil in a pan.

Add chopped garlic and stir. This will infuse the aroma of garlic in the oil.

Add chopped mushrooms and salt immediately to draw out all the moisture from the mushrooms.

Cook until the water dries and the mushrooms turn golden.

Add the chilli flakes.

Add the reserved water to the mushrooms and garlic and bring to a boil. This is the sauce for the pasta.

Add the juice from one small lemon to it.

Lower the heat, add salt to taste and let the sauce simmer for about 5 minutes till the liquid is reduced by about a third.

Now add the pasta to the mix and coat it in the sauce.

Add the basil and parsley.

Top it with the lemon rind.

Serve hot.

❝Simple and quick to cook, this is a great dish to bring for lunch as it works well even when eaten cold. By adding the right veggies you can have a wholesome dish with a great balance of carbohydrates, protein and fibre. ❞

Yasmin Karachiwala's

Quinoa Stir-Fry

⟳ HIGH PROTEIN

One taste of celebrity nutritionist and trainer Yasmin Karachiwala's veggie-filled, high-protein quinoa stir-fry cooked in coconut oil will convince you that healthy foods can also be delicious.

Ingredients

3 tbsp raw quinoa

1 cup water

2 cups mixed vegetables (broccoli, mushrooms, red and yellow peppers, carrot)

30 g tofu

Salt to taste

Pepper to taste

1 tbsp coconut oil

1 tsp apple cider vinegar

½ tsp liquid aminos or soy sauce (liquid aminos is a healthier substitute for soy sauce)

Preparation

Boil the quinoa in 1 cup of water.

Heat the coconut oil in a pan.

Add the vegetables and stir.

Add salt and pepper.

Add the quinoa.

After 2 minutes of stirring, add the apple cider vinegar and liquid aminos/soy sauce.

Give a toss and add the tofu. Cook for 2–3 minutes.

Serve hot.

❝*Healthy eating should be a lifestyle and not just a quick fix! I try to get most of my nutrition from the foods I eat instead of popping pills for it.*❞

Sarita Tanwar's

Sweet Corn Pulao

Don't be fooled by its simplicity – producer Sarita Tanwar's sweet corn pulao smells enticing, and tastes even better.

Ingredients

2 cups basmati rice

1 cup sweet corn

2 green chillies, slit

1 tsp cumin seeds

1 tsp paprika powder

2 medium-sized tomatoes, finely chopped

2 tbsp mint leaves

Salt to taste

2 tbsp oil

4½ cups water

Preparation

Wash and soak the rice in 4½ cups of water for 15 minutes.

Heat oil in a pan.

Add the cumin seeds and green chillies.

After 5–10 seconds, add the tomatoes and sauté for 3–4 minutes.

Add paprika powder and sweet corn to this mixture.

After 1 minute add the rice, water and mint leaves.

Bring to a boil on high flame.

Then reduce the flame and cook till done.

Serve with curd, green chutney or salsa.

"*It's a simple and delicious recipe. Given that we are all bored with cooking the usual dishes, this one doesn't need a lot of preparation or cook time.*"

Sonali Bendre's

Sweet Potato Khichdi

Fuss-free and loved by all, this twist on the typical sabudana khichdi is an extension of actor Sonali Bendre's cheerful personality.

Ingredients

2 sweet potatoes, boiled and diced

1 cup roasted and ground peanuts

2 tbsp olive oil

½ tsp cumin seeds

½ tsp mustard seeds

5–6 curry leaves

2 green chillies, finely chopped

2 tbsp grated coconut

A handful of finely chopped coriander

Salt to taste

Preparation

Heat olive oil in a pan.

Add the cumin and mustard seeds.

Once they begin to crackle, add the green chillies and curry leaves.

To this add the peanuts.

Next, add the sweet potatoes and salt to taste.

Mix well.

Garnish with coconut and coriander and serve.

"*As they say, you are what you eat! And my mantra has always been not to measure my food but instead watch what I eat.* **"**

Shikhar Dhawan's

Rava Masala Uttappam

🍽 **BREAKFAST**

Give your breakfast a lift with a power-packed rava uttappam like the one Shikhar Dhawan kick-starts his day with. Want kids to eat it? Just tell them it's what their favourite cricketers devour for breakfast.

Ingredients

1 cup rava

2 cups water

1 onion, finely chopped

2 carrots, grated

1 capsicum, finely chopped

2–3 green chillies, finely chopped

Salt to taste

4 tbsp oil

Preparation

Soak the rava in water and keep overnight.

The next day, add the vegetables and salt to taste.

Heat 1 tbsp oil in a pan.

Spread the batter like a pancake on it.

Cook evenly on both sides for 2–3 minutes each.

Serve with sambar and coconut chutney.

❝*This carb-loaded breakfast keeps my energy up the whole day!*❞

Malaika Arora's

Zucchini Noodles with Red Bell Pepper Sauce

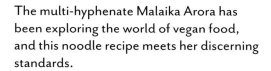 VEGAN

The multi-hyphenate Malaika Arora has been exploring the world of vegan food, and this noodle recipe meets her discerning standards.

Ingredients

2 zucchinis

2 tbsp olive oil

2 garlic cloves, crushed

2 red bell peppers, chopped

Oregano to taste

Salt to taste

Preparation

Skin the zucchinis and cut them lengthwise into thin strips.

In a pan, heat olive oil and add the garlic, oregano and red bell peppers and sauté till soft.

Add the zucchini and salt and sauté for a minute.

Remove from heat and serve with a lime wedge.

❝*One of my favourite dishes in my quest to eat healthy and vegan!*❞

Mohit Savargaonkar's

Tofu Curry

He is the chef responsible for making sure your favourite Bollywood stars stick to their diets. And as you can see from this recipe, Mohit Savargaonkar ensures that it's never all work and no play.

Ingredients

85 g tofu
8–10 garlic cloves, finely chopped
1-inch ginger, finely chopped
5 asparagus sticks, roughly chopped
1 cup chopped shimeji mushrooms
1 cup chopped broccoli
½ cup chopped red bell pepper
Sesame oil
3 tbsp chilli bean sauce
2 tsp soy sauce
Water
2 tbsp chopped spring onions
1 tbsp sesame seeds

Preparation

Heat sesame oil in a pan. Add 1 tbsp ginger and 1 tbsp garlic.
Add the chilli bean sauce and stir.
Add the soy sauce and ½ cup water. Cook for 5 minutes.

In a separate pan, heat 3 tbsp sesame oil. Add 1 tbsp ginger and 1 tbsp garlic. Add the mushrooms, bell pepper and broccoli and stir.

Add 2 tbsp water to this mix and toss the vegetables for 1 minute. Keep aside.

Add the tofu to the sauce and cook for 2–3 minutes.

In a bowl, ladle the vegetables first. Top with the tofu mix and garnish with some spring onions and sesame seeds.

"My favourite thing about this dish is that it's SIMPLE! It has multiple textures and a distinctive umami flavour.

Snack dabba

Hunting for something to curb
that 4 p.m. junk food craving?
We've got flavour bombs for every palate.

Akshay Kumar's

Avocado Toast

The actor gives this millennial favourite
a desi twist, with chatpata chaat masala
playing off the sweetness of fresh
pomegranate pearls.

Ingredients

1 ripe avocado

*2 slices of multigrain
bread*

1 tbsp olive oil

½ tsp Himalayan pink salt

½ tsp chaat masala

Pomegranate pearls

Preparation

In a bowl, mash the ripe avocado.

Add olive oil, a pinch of Himalayan pink
salt and a pinch of chaat masala.

Mix all these together.

Slather this on slices of toasted bread.

Garnish with pomegranate pearls.

❝*Eating clean is not an option but a way of life for me.***❞**

Eeshan Kashyap's

Zero-Waste Bread Loaf

Your nani will approve of food entrepreneur Eeshan Kashyap's cooking mantra: don't let anything go to waste.

Ingredients

2½ cups all-purpose flour

3 tbsp brown sugar

3 tbsp fresh yeast

1 tbsp salt

½ cup day-old boiled rice

5 tbsp milk

1 cup water

5 tbsp chopped chives

Mixed seeds for topping

Pre-preparation

Mix the brown sugar with warm water and fresh yeast. Keep aside for at least 10 minutes to activate the yeast.

Preparation

Mix the flour and salt.

Once you see it bubbling, add the activated yeast mixture into the flour mix, along with rice, chives and milk.

Knead the dough using your hands and make a lumpy, dry ball.

Keep this dough aside in a bowl covered with a wet kitchen towel for the dough to rise and the yeast to activate.

After resting the dough for at least 20 minutes, you will observe it has doubled in size.

Punch and knead again, and this time rest it for only 10 minutes.

The dough will rise again. Divide it into two equal parts and roll each one into a round loaf.

You can make a round dough loaf or place in a dish of any shape to prove (i.e. rise again).

Knead tightly and place in an aluminium baking tin.

Add mixed seeds of your choice on top and allow to rest for at least 25 minutes again.

Preheat the oven at 175 °C.

Bake the bread for exactly 25 minutes in the oven on even heat.

You will see a nice golden-brown loaf.

Rest it for 2 hours.

> *I call this a zero-waste recipe because I make it with boiled rice left over from the previous night's dinner. It's a delicious bread loaf and lasts for at least four days when refrigerated.*

Sophie Choudry's

Quinoa and Sweet Potato Cutlets

⊛ **HIGH PROTEIN**

When your carb cravings kick into high gear, actor Sophie Choudry's vegetarian cutlet recipe will satiate you.

Ingredients

½ cup quinoa

2 sweet potatoes, boiled and mashed

2 tbsp roasted chana powder

1 tbsp roasted kasuri methi

2 green chillies, finely chopped

½ tsp grated ginger

½ tsp red chilli powder

½ tsp cumin powder

½ tsp ground pepper

½ tsp chaat masala

2 cups water

5–6 tbsp oil

Preparation

Soak the quinoa for 2–3 hours and then boil it for 2–3 minutes till it fluffs up.

Keep aside to cool.

Add the sweet potatoes, green chillies, ginger, red chilli powder, cumin powder, black pepper and a pinch of chaat masala.

Add the chana powder and kasuri methi to this mix.

Mix it all together and make small tikkis out of it.

Keep in the refrigerator for 1 hour so that the tikkis firm up.

Smear oil on a pan. Fry the tikkis in the pan till they are golden on both sides.

Serve with a chutney of your choice.

❝*I'm not vegetarian or vegan, but I try to eat plant-based meals at least twice a week, and on those days this dish is one of my favourites.* ❞

Smita Deo's

Cheesy Vegetable Cutlets

🏈 KID-FRIENDLY

Crispy on the outside, gooey on the inside, food blogger Smita Deo's veggie extravaganza really hits the spot.

Ingredients

1 cup crumbled cottage cheese

1 cup boiled, peeled and mashed potatoes

1 cup boiled corn niblets

1 cup boiled fresh peas

1 cup boiled and peeled carrots, chopped into small pieces

1 medium-sized red bell pepper, finely chopped

4–5 green chillies, finely chopped

¼ tsp pepper powder

¼ tsp garam masala

1 tsp amchur

Salt to taste

1 cup breadcrumbs

Oil for frying

Preparation

In a bowl mix all the ingredients, except the oil and breadcrumbs.

Make small cutlets with the mixture.

Coat the cutlets with breadcrumbs.

Heat a pan and fry the cutlets so they are crisp and golden on both sides.

Serve with ketchup or chutney.

❝*This is a perfect dish to enjoy with a cuppa tea on those rainy days.* ❞

Swagata Chatterjee's

Dim'er Devil

Home chef Swagata Chatterjee's dim'er devil gives a fishy spin to this crispy snack by adding some prawns. As it turns out, you can't take fish out of Bengal's chai-time snack either!

Ingredients

6 eggs, boiled

2 potatoes, boiled

1 onion

1 tbsp grated ginger

1 green chilli, finely chopped

2 carrots, grated

2 sprigs coriander, chopped

12 small prawns, fried

8 tbsp sunflower oil

½ cup breadcrumbs

Salt to taste

For the batter

1 egg

Salt to taste

For the garnishing

1 cucumber, chopped

1 tomato, chopped

1 onion, chopped

Preparation

Mash the potatoes with salt, onion, ginger, green chilli, coriander leaves and grated carrot.

Slice the eggs in half.

Top one half with the mashed potato and place a fried prawn on top.

Join the two halves of the egg to make it look like a whole egg.

Dip it in the batter and then roll it in the breadcrumbs. Repeat twice.

Refrigerate for 2 hours.

Fry them till they turn golden brown.

Sprinkle salt, garnish and serve.

> "*The British call them scotch eggs, Americans know them as devilled eggs, but in Bengali households they are called dim'er devil. This crunchy snack is rich in protein, the mashed potatoes take care of your fibre intake, and the 'devil' pairs eggcelently with chai, coffee and even alcohol.*"

Aalika Banerjee's

Lettuce and Avocado Hung Curd Salad

Nutritionist Aalika Banerjee's salad recipe is the perfect trio of creamy, crunchy and sour, guaranteed to satisfy diet junkies and carb loaders alike.

Ingredients

1 avocado

1 cup lettuce

½ cup parmesan cheese

5 tsp extra virgin olive oil

2 onions

5 tsp feta cheese

3 garlic cloves, crushed

A handful of pine nuts/walnuts

½ cup cherry tomatoes

A handful of pumpkin seeds

¼ cup paneer

1 cup hung curd

Juice of 1 lemon

½ tsp sugar

Salt to taste

Pepper to taste

Preparation

Hang fresh curd in a muslin cloth for 4–5 hours till all the water drains away.

Taste the curd. If it's already sour, skip adding the lemon, if not, add 3–4 drops of lemon juice.

Add salt, pepper and crushed garlic.

Then slowly emulsify the curd by adding olive oil and whisking till you get a smooth dressing.

Melt butter in a pan and add the chopped onions. Cook till brown. Add ½ tsp sugar. The onions should be caramelized.

Cook the paneer in a pan till brown on both sides.

Season with salt and pepper.

Toss the lettuce with the dressing.

Rest it for 5 minutes.

To the lettuce, add the avocado, onion, feta cheese, cherry tomatoes, paneer and crushed walnuts/pine nuts.

Toss until well combined. Garnish with shaved parmesan and a few pumpkin seeds.

❝*I've always been a lover of salads because there's so much to play around with. The hung curd dressing is super creamy and the fibre content makes this salad very filling.* ❞

Surabhi Sehgal's

Roasted Pumpkin and Turmeric Hummus

⟳ **HIGH PROTEIN**

Scooped on to pita chips, layered into a sandwich or devoured with fresh carrot sticks, there's no wrong way to eat food blogger Surabhi Sehgal's 4 p.m. snack.

Ingredients

2 cups peeled and cubed pumpkin

1 cup boiled chickpeas

2 tbsp tahini

1 tbsp lemon juice

3–4 garlic cloves

½ tsp turmeric

Salt to taste

3 tbsp olive oil

Aquafaba if needed

Preparation

Coat the pumpkin cubes with turmeric, a little salt and a tbsp of olive oil.

Preheat the oven at 200 °C.

Spread the pumpkin cubes on a baking tray and bake in the oven for 20–25 minutes until they are soft and light brown in colour.

Let them cool.

In a blender add roasted pumpkin, chickpeas, garlic, tahini, olive oil, lime juice and salt to taste. Blend to a fine paste.

Add some aquafaba if needed.

Transfer to a bowl and let it chill in the refrigerator for a couple of hours.

Top this with some nuts, herbs and a drizzle of olive oil.

Serve with crackers or vegetable sticks of your choice.

❝*This hummus tastes like magic to my Indian taste buds. Velvety, sweet and nutty, with the tartness from the lime juice making this a beautifully balanced dish.* ❞

Maria Goretti's

Beetroot Salad

Trust TV personality Maria Goretti to turn one of the most controversial vegetables – beetroot – into an international crowd-pleaser.

Courtesy Zene Zoe Warsi

Ingredients

1 beetroot, boiled

1 orange, peeled

½ cup cherry tomatoes

¼ cup baby spinach

2 tbsp mustard microgreens

2 tbsp feta cheese

1½ tbsp mixed seeds

1 tbsp extra virgin olive oil

½ tsp balsamic vinegar

Squeeze of lime

Preparation

In a bowl, mix beetroot, cherry tomatoes, baby spinach and orange.

To this add extra virgin olive oil, balsamic vinegar and a squeeze of lime and mix.

Garnish with feta cheese, mixed seeds and mustard microgreens.

❝*The citrus in this salad gives you a burst of flavours and puts you in a lovely holiday mood. I change the fruits seasonally, and it's one of my favourite salads.*❞

Anjali Mukherjee's

Chop-and-Mix Salad

🌾 **HEALTHY GRAIN**

On manic Mondays, when you have five minutes to spare between deadlines, appointments and work emails, nutritionist Anjali Mukherjee's chop-and-mix salad will boost your mood.

Ingredients

1 pomegranate

1 apple

2 carrots

2 cucumbers

6 tsp feta cheese

4 tbsp whole millet, boiled and salted (optional)

10 rocket leaves (optional)

Preparation

Chop all the ingredients and mix together in a large bowl. Crumble the feta cheese over this and toss.

It's ready to be served.

❝❝*I love this salad because my definition of food is something that nourishes you. My primary objective is to use the healing property of specific foods. I have tried to bring about a balance between taste and health in this recipe.* **❞❞**

Sarah Dacosta's

Rustic Spinach Chicken Soup

If masking is self-care in beauty, sipping on soup is its food equivalent. Film-maker Sara Dacosta's warm, comforting rustic chicken soup is both for the body and the soul.

Ingredients

3 large onions, coarsely chopped

1 bay leaf

2–3 cloves

2 tomatoes, finely chopped

4–5 garlic cloves

2 large potatoes, chopped into cubes

5 cups chicken stock or 2 vegetable stock cubes

500 g chicken breast, cut into thin strips

3 tbsp freshly ground pepper

1 large bunch of spinach, roughly chopped

Salt to taste

2 tbsp butter

Preparation

In a large soup pan, add the butter, bay leaf and cloves.

Wait till you can smell the aromas of the spices. Then add the garlic and fry till it browns a little.

Add the onions and cook till slightly translucent.

Add the tomatoes and cook till slightly mushy.

Add the potatoes.

Add the chicken stock; if you are a vegetarian, use vegetable stock cubes.

Let the potatoes cook.

Add the chicken breast.

Then add the spinach leaves and pepper and cook for not more than 5 minutes or till the spinach turns into a darker green.

Serve with a nice crusty bread.

❝*This soup is comfort food for me. I make it when I'm sick or when it's cold. It's filling, super healthy and full of rainy-day memories of cooking with Mom.* ❞

Shefali Shah's

Creamy Vegetable Soup

🏷️ KID-FRIENDLY

Actor Shefali Shah's greatest performance till date? Convincing her kids to slurp up the healthiest vegetables she can find, and leaving them asking for seconds.

Ingredients

1 cup chopped cabbage

1 cup diced cauliflower

½ zucchini, diced

1 bottle gourd, diced

1 cup button mushrooms

4–5 garlic cloves

1 bay leaf

1 tsp peppercorns

1 cinnamon stick

2 sprigs parsley

2 tbsp oil

3 cups water

Salt to taste

Preparation

Heat the oil in a pressure cooker.

Add the bay leaf, peppercorns and cinnamon and stir till they begin to release their aromas.

Add the cabbage, cauliflower, bottle gourd and zucchini and stir.

Add salt to taste.

Add 2 cups of water and pressure cook for 2 whistles.

Let it cool and then puree it in a mixer grinder.

In a separate pan, sauté mushrooms till they release water and turn golden.

Add the puree.

Add some freshly chopped parsley and serve hot.

💬 *I make this cream of fool-your-kids soup because it's nutritious and has all the veggies they won't normally eat. You can make it as a soup or use it as a puree for pasta or risotto, and it tastes great.* 💬

Cheat dabba

The incurable Indian sweet tooth
meets its match with healthy tweaks
on the most sinful treats.

Pooja Dhingra's

Chocolate Cardamom Cookie

Chef Dhingra's cookies are the perfect reward (or bribe) to give your family members to finish their chores and all the veggies on their plates. Yup, even karela.

Ingredients

¼ cup ghee

¼ cup powdered sugar

¼ cup all-purpose flour

1 tbsp cocoa powder

½ tsp cardamom powder

Almond flakes to decorate

Preparation

In a bowl, whisk the ghee, sugar and cardamom powder till light and creamy.

In another bowl, sift the flour and cocoa powder.

Add the flour mixture to the ghee mixture and use your hands to make a dough.

Portion the dough into small balls, flatten them and place on a baking tray lined with parchment paper/foil.

Sprinkle the almond flakes on top of the cookies.

Bake in a preheated oven at 165 °C for 15–18 minutes.

❝This recipe is inspired by the nankhatais we used to eat when we were growing up. It's incredibly easy to make, a great recipe to bake with kids and the perfect snack for your dabba. ❞

Chandrima Sarkar's

Chocolate Almond Cake

🥜 NUTS INCLUDED

Chocolate cake, like peace and harmony, is something the world needs more of. And food blogger Chandrima Sarkar's favourite recipe will win over even your most stubborn opponent.

Ingredients

¾ cup all-purpose flour

¼ cup unsweetened cocoa powder

1 tsp baking powder

¼ tsp salt

¾ cup brown/white caster sugar

1 tsp vanilla extract

2 eggs

½ cup olive oil/vegetable oil

¼ cup chopped almonds + some for sprinkling on top

¼ cup chocolate chips + some for sprinkling on top

Preparation

Ensure all ingredients are at room temperature.

Preheat the oven at 180 °C. Grease a 7.5-inch cake pan and line with baking paper.

In a bowl, mix the flour, cocoa powder, baking powder, salt and sugar.

Next, add the eggs, oil and vanilla extract. Whisk until a smooth, lump-free batter forms. Do not whisk for longer.

Mix in almonds and chocolate chips. Pour the batter into the cake pan.

Tap the pan gently on the kitchen counter a couple of times to release the air bubbles. Sprinkle some almonds and chocolate chips on top.

Bake for 40–45 minutes. Check the cake after the first 30 minutes of baking by inserting a sharp knife in the middle.

The cake is ready if the knife comes out clean. If not, bake it for a few more minutes and then check again.

Cool the cake in the pan for 10 minutes and then run a sharp knife around the edges of the pan and carefully remove the cake. Turn it on to a cooling rack.

Once cooled, slice, serve and enjoy!

Notes

Baking time may vary a little bit for different ovens and different sizes of baking pans.

During baking when the cake browns perfectly on top (after 30 minutes or so), cover the top loosely with a piece of aluminium foil until the cake is fully baked. This helps in preventing over-browning on the top.

Store the cake slices in an airtight container and refrigerate; consume within a week.

❝A simple and healthy recipe loved by my young daughter and husband alike. This one is a crowd-pleaser!❞

Neha Sethi's

Dark Chocolate Tart with Sea Salt

Dark chocolate and sea salt, a combination so tempting it should be illegal. And chef Neha Sethi's version is impossible to resist.

Ingredients

For the shell

10 tbsp butter (room temperature)

½ cup caster sugar

2 large eggs

2 cups flour

1 tsp salt

For the chocolate ganache

1 cup chopped bittersweet chocolate

A pinch of sea salt

1½ cups cream

½ tsp instant coffee powder

Preparation

For the tart shell

Cream together the butter and sugar until fluffy.

Add the eggs and mix until just incorporated.

Add the flour and salt and mix slowly to make a dough.

Wrap in plastic and refrigerate for at least 1 hour or overnight.

After removing from the refrigerator, roll out the dough between two sheets of butter paper. It should be round, a little larger than a 9-inch tart pan, and about ¼ inch thick.

Press it into a well-greased 9-inch tart pan lined with butter or butter paper and trim the excess dough.

Place the shell in the freezer until ready to bake.

Preheat the oven at 175 °C.

Line the tart shell with butter paper and fill with dried beans or pie weights.

Bake for 30 minutes. Remove the paper and weights. Bake for another 10 minutes.

Allow to cool while you make the chocolate filling.

For the ganache

Place the chocolate and salt in a heatproof bowl.

Heat the cream till it comes to a boil. Then pour it over the chocolate and let it sit for 3 minutes.

Add the coffee powder.

Whisk the chocolate into the cream.

Pour the ganache into the tart shell and allow to set at room temperature.

Alternatively, it can be kept in the refrigerator to set.

Sprinkle with sea salt before serving.

* In case you do not have a tart pan, you can use a cake tin with a removable bottom. If doing so, give the tart a height of about 1 inch by taking the dough up along the side of the pan and trimming it at a 1 inch height.

❝*This dish is special to me because it reminds me that a straightforward technique and great ingredients can still be more than the sum of their parts. It's comfort food at its best!*❞

Rachel Goenka's

Sweet Potato and Chocolate Cake

Pastry chef Rachel Goenka's Instagram feed is a dangerous place for calorie counters. But this sweet potato cake – packed with vitamins and minerals – is a happy compromise.

Ingredients

¼ cup butter

1 tbsp Sugar Free

4 egg yolks

¼ cup sugar-free chocolate

½ cup mashed sweet potato

1¼ cup flour

2 egg whites

For the sauce

¼ cup sugar-free chocolate

¼ cup cream

¼ cup milk

Preparation

Melt the chocolate and butter and add the mashed potato.

Make a mixture with the egg yolks and Sugar Free and fold into the chocolate mixture.

Whip the egg whites and fold into the chocolate and egg batter and add flour.

Bake at 200 °C for 15 minutes.

Serve with warm sauce.

Preparation

For the sauce, warm the milk and cream in a saucepan.

Add the sugar-free chocolate to this cream mixture and mix gently.

❝This sweet potato cake is absolutely delicious and healthy, too! You can bake this in a square tin and cut it up into squares for a healthy alternative whenever the chocolate cravings hit!❞

Tarana Mav's

Chocolate Dhokla

Gujarati delicacies are famous for catering to those with a sweet tooth, sometimes halfway through the main course. This chocolate-flavoured decadent farsan from home chef turned 'mompreneur' Tarana Mav will definitely keep you and the kids coming back for more.

Ingredients

For the dhokla batter

1 cup rava

Juice of 1 lemon

1 tsp baking powder

2 tsp sugar

5 tbsp melted chocolate (dark or regular)

1 tbsp oil

1 tsp Eno fruit salt

Water

For the chocolate syrup

4 tbsp melted chocolate

2 tbsp milk

4 tbsp sugar syrup

Directions

Mix rava, lemon juice, baking powder, sugar and oil in a bowl.

Add ¾ cup water and mix well till you have a soft batter.

Keep aside for a while.

Prepare the boiler with some hot water.

Grease a baking tray with oil.

Add fruit salt to the batter. Mix thoroughly.

Put half of this mix in a small baking tray. Then add a layer of chocolate syrup. Add the remaining half of the batter on top of the chocolate syrup layer and keep in the boiler.

Cover and boil for 15–20 minutes on high flame.

To check if it is ready, stick a knife in the dhokla.

If the knife is clean when you pull it out, the dhokla is ready. If not, let it boil for some more time.

After it's cooked, let it cool for 10 minutes.

Cut it into the desired shape and plate. Pour some hot chocolate syrup on it and serve.

> **"**Lately, I've been experimenting more – I go to the kitchen, collect all the random ingredients I have and try to make an innovative dish combining those ingredients only. That's how I came up with chocolate dhokla. **"**

Alka Hiranandani's

Rum Cake

🔗 **NUTS INCLUDED**   ✹ **GLUTEN-FREE**

Even Akshay Kumar can't say no to a second helping of this rich gluten-free cake, especially when made by his entrepreneur sister, Alka Hiranandani.

Ingredients

½ cup oil

100 g jaggery

2 bananas

¼ cup yogurt

1 cup sorghum flour

½ cup almond milk

¼ cup rum

½ tsp baking soda

1 tsp baking powder

¼ tsp cinnamon powder

¼ tsp salt

10 walnuts, chopped

2 dates, chopped

60 g chocolate chips or any dark chocolate

10–12 golden raisins

Preparation

Grease a baking tray with oil. Dust some sorghum flour on it and keep aside.

Mix the dates, raisins and 2 tbsp sorghum flour in a bowl and keep aside.

In another bowl, put oil, jaggery and yogurt and mix till smooth and creamy.

Place a sieve on top of the mixer. Add sorghum flour, baking powder, baking soda, salt and cinnamon powder and sieve well to get rid of any lumps. Then add the milk and mix well.

Now mix the nuts with the remaining flour.

Then mash the bananas in the paste.

Add the chocolate chips or dark chocolate.

Add the rum and mix well.

Pour the batter into the tray and level it with a spatula.

Add the chopped almonds.

Bake in the oven for 30–35 minutes at 180 °C.

> ❝I've seen Tweak India go from an idea scribbled on a piece of paper in my sister-in-law's overflowing diary to a living, breathing entity. To celebrate its first anniversary, here's a walnut banana rum cake that's a big hit at all our family parties. ❞

Suvir Saran's

Doughnuts

Get ready to be everyone's favourite party host with this recipe for chef Suvir Saran's divine doughnuts.

Ingredients

3 cups canola oil

2 cups all-purpose flour + extra
for dusting work surface

1½ tsp baking powder

½ tsp salt

½ tsp ground ginger

½ tsp freshly grated nutmeg

¼ tsp cinnamon

1 large egg

½ cup plain yogurt

2½ cups sugar

Zest of 1 lemon

½ tsp baking soda

Preparation

Fill 3 inches of a medium-sized saucepan with the oil and heat to 180 °C.

Sift the flour, baking powder, salt, ginger, nutmeg and cinnamon into a large bowl.

In a medium-sized bowl, whisk together the egg, yogurt, ½ cup sugar and lemon zest.

Add the baking soda and whisk to combine (the mixture should get bubbly).

Add the yogurt mixture to the dry ingredients and stir to combine.

Put the remaining sugar on a large plate or in a baking dish and set aside.

Sprinkle a generous amount of flour on to your work surface. Transfer the dough ball to it and sprinkle flour over it. Pat it with your hands into a thin disc. It should be ¼ to ⅓ inch thick.

Use a 2- to 3-inch-wide cookie cutter (or upturned coffee mug) to cut circles out of the dough. Use a 1-inch cookie cutter (or bottle cap) to cut out small circles from the centre of each larger dough disc.

Place the doughnut shapes on a plate and pat the remaining dough into a large disc, cutting out doughnuts as described.

Fry 2 to 4 doughnuts at a time, turning and basting often, for 2 to 2½ minutes, or until they're evenly browned all over.

Place the hot doughnuts in the reserved sugar and flip to coat the other side.

Eat while hot or within a couple of hours of frying.

"Doughnuts bring back some of my fondest childhood memories, with mom throwing this dough together in minutes, and us kids gobbling up the sugar-tossed doughnuts as quickly as she made them."

Sherry Malhotra's

Kaddu ka Halwa

🏷 **NUTS INCLUDED**

What do Cinderella and home chef Sherry Malhotra have in common? They both understand the magical powers of the underrated pumpkin.

Ingredients

2½ cups washed, peeled and grated kaddu (yellow pumpkin)

½ cup sugar

2–3 tbsp ghee

3 cups full cream milk

5 tsp chopped cashew nuts

10–12 almonds, chopped

10–12 pistachios, chopped

5 tsp raisins

5 tsp pumpkin seeds

½ tsp powdered cardamom

Preparation

Boil milk in a saucepan. We have to thicken the milk, so keep cooking it on medium flame, stirring every now and then.

Put ghee in a pan, followed by the pumpkin.

Roast on low flame for a couple of minutes.

Cover the pan and cook on low flame for 10 minutes till soft. Simultaneously, keep stirring the milk in the saucepan.

Add sugar to the softened pumpkin and mix.

Cook while stirring continuously.

By now the boiling milk has thickened and looks like khoya. Add it to the pumpkin mash.

Cook on high flame for a few minutes.

Add half of the cashew nuts, raisins, pumpkin seeds, almonds and cardamom powder and mix.

Cook for about a minute, stirring continuously.

Transfer to a bowl and garnish with chopped cashews, pistachios and almonds before serving.

"*A delicious way of disguising pumpkin and making it more kid-friendly!*"

Rhea Mitra Dalal's

Aam'er Luchi

Juicy mango, fragrant ghee, soft chhenna –
food entrepreneur Rhea Mitra Dalal's
Bengali treat will convince you that summer
vacations last forever.

Ingredients

2 cups all-purpose flour

2 tsp ghee

2 tbsp chhenna (curd cheese)

¾ cup mango pulp

1 cup fresh coconut milk

Ghee for frying

Preparation

To make the dough for the luchis, start by incorporating the curd
cheese into the flour.

Mash the curd cheese as finely as you can with your fingers, flattening
the granules as much as possible.

Add flour (a little at a time) to the curd cheese and keep mixing and
kneading till all the flour is used up. You will end up with a crumbly
mixture.

The curd cheese must mix with the flour well so you ultimately have a
smooth and lump-free dough.

Once the curd cheese is well incorporated, add the ghee and mix it in
properly.

Next, add the mango pulp.

Once the mango pulp is mixed in, add the coconut milk and knead till you have a soft dough.

Make balls of the dough and roll out luchis around 6 inches in diameter.

Heat ghee in a kadhai and fry the luchis. The hot ghee will ensure your luchis fluff up nicely.

> **"***I have started studying Bengali food seriously in the last few years, trying to learn as much as I can from every available source. This is one of the recipes I discovered in that quest and is now a favourite.***"**

Anupama Menon's

Oats Pancakes

🌾 HEALTHY GRAIN   ⊙ BREAKFAST

✎ KID-FRIENDLY

Sweet yogurt cream and honey dotted with
berries and slathered over a golden-brown
pancake – nutritionist Anupama Menon has
just introduced us to her preferred form of
morning meditation.

Ingredients

5 tbsp powdered oats

3 tbsp powdered poha

2 tbsp whole wheat flour

4 tsp jaggery

½ tsp chia seeds

1 tbsp powdered almonds

1 egg

Milk as required

½ tsp baking soda

1 cup berries of choice, dried/fresh

1 banana

4 tbsp butter

For the probiotic cream

½ cup thick yogurt

2 tsp honey

3 drops vanilla essence

Preparation

For the pancakes

Beat the egg with a fork.

Mix the powdered oats, poha, wheat flour, almond powder and baking soda.

Add the egg and ¼ cup milk.

Mix till lump-free.

Add the chia seeds and jaggery.

Now add enough milk for it to have a pancake-batter-like consistency.

Heat the griddle and put 1 tsp butter.

Spoon the batter but don't spread too much; it needs to be slightly thick.

Cover and cook for 30–40 seconds. Flip over and ensure the pancake has cooked well.

Serve with berries, banana and probiotic cream.

For the probiotic cream

Hang the curd in a muslin cloth until the water drains out.

Spoon into a bowl and add honey.

Beat well and add the essence.

Mix well and refrigerate until ready to serve.

❝ *This dish is healthy and fun, especially when you add different flavours of fruits, berries and seeds. Kids love it, it's easy to prepare and for those who aren't great at cooking like me, you'll feel like you've earned your chef's hat for once.* ❞

Maheep Kapoor's

Overnight-Soaked Oats

🌾 **HEALTHY GRAIN**　　⊙ **BREAKFAST**

Jewellery designer Maheep Kapoor's overnight oats will help you get one step closer to breakfasting in bed – just add the toppings of your choice (jam, chocolate flakes, almonds) to the soaked oats, vanilla extract and milk mix. Running late? Assemble it in a jar and you have breakfast (or a snack) on the go.

Ingredients

½ cup rolled oats

½ cup almond milk

¼ tsp vanilla extract

1 tbsp honey

1 tbsp strawberry jam

1 tbsp peanut butter

1 tbsp almond flakes

2 tbsp banana

1 tsp chocolate flakes

Preparation

Mix the oats, vanilla extract and milk in a bowl.

Keep in the refrigerator overnight.

In the morning, add honey and toppings of your choice (strawberry jam, peanut butter, almonds flakes, banana, chocolate flakes).

Serve chilled.

❝*An extremely easy and healthy recipe. I love having overnight-soaked oats with different toppings!*❞

Monalisa Mohapatra's

Jamun Popsicles

Home-made popsicles will instantly turn you into the favourite parent. Little do the kids know how simple it is to make these preservative-free ice creams by food blogger Monalisa Mohapatra. Jamun can be replaced by any fresh seasonal fruit.

Ingredients

1 cup jamun

1 tbsp rock salt

1 lemon

2 tbsp sugar

½ cup water

Preparation

Deseed the jamuns and put them in a mixer grinder along with rock salt, a dash of lemon and sugar.

Blend everything together with water.

Pour this mixture into popsicle moulds and freeze.

Once frozen, serve them with a sprinkle of rock salt.

❝ *'Be careful when you are eating jamuns – don't stain your clothes,' my grandmother would say. But we monkeys would make a mess and come back with purple tongues and stained clothes after having jamuns to our hearts' content.* ❞

Swayampurna Mishra Singh's

Cinnamon Rolls

Sugar, spice and everything nice – the food blogger promises these fluffy clouds of heaven will disappear down hungry throats faster than you can think.

Ingredients

2 cups all-purpose flour

3 tbsp water at 43 °C

½ tsp active dry yeast

1 tbsp sugar

½ tbsp lukewarm milk

¼ cup sugar

1 tsp vanilla extract

Half of ⅓ cup melted butter

1 egg

For the filling

½ cup dark brown sugar

¼ cup softened butter

1 tbsp cinnamon powder

For the cream cheese frosting

1 pack of Philadelphia cream cheese

¼ cup butter

1 cup powdered sugar

1 tsp bourbon vanilla extract

Preparation

Making the dough

Activate the yeast by heating water at 43 °C and then adding the yeast and sugar to it.

Mix and leave aside for about 5 minutes till it's activated and frothy.

In a mixing bowl, add flour and a pinch of salt.

In another bowl, mix together egg and sugar.

Add melted butter (ensure it's cool before you add it to the egg), milk and vanilla and whisk together till well mixed.

Now add the activated yeast mixture and give it a quick gentle mix.

Pour this liquid into the bowl with the flour.

Just mix it up with a spatula till it comes together. No kneading required. It should be a very sticky dough.

Cover the bowl with a kitchen towel and leave the dough to rise in a warm place for 1½ hours.

Rolling it out

After the dough has risen to almost double the volume, transfer to your countertop and knock down the air.

Then gently roll it out into a 16x7-inch rectangle.

Brush the softened butter all over it and sprinkle the filling mixture (the sugar and cinnamon should have been mixed beforehand).

Leave a ½-inch border along the dough without filling.

Now starting from the end closest to you, roll the dough into a nice tight log.

Use a sharp knife or pastry cutter to cut it into 9–10 equal-sized rolls.

Place them on a baking tray lined with parchment. Leave a space of 2–3 inches between them.

Cover and let the rolls rise for 30 minutes.

Bake in a 180 °C preheated oven for 20–25 minutes. Don't overbake!

Remove and immediately brush a little frosting on the rolls. This keeps them extra moist.

Once the rolls cool down, spread the frosting over them liberally and serve.

> *I chose this dish because it's my daughter's absolute favourite! It's very versatile, so if I am out of brown sugar I use raspberry jam and almond flakes for the filling and top it with white chocolate frosting!*

Saransh Goila's

Rajgira Sheera with Ghee Roast Apple

 **HEALTHY GRAIN**

Antioxidant-rich amaranth is having its moment in the spotlight, and what better way to savour it than with chef Saransh Goila's (@saranshgoila) tweak to our childhood staple snack.

Ingredients

1 cup rajgira flour (amaranth flour)

½ cup ghee

100 g jaggery

1 cup water

1½ cups milk

A pinch of cardamom powder

2–3 strands saffron

1 apple

2 tbsp sugar

10–12 walnuts

10–12 black raisins

Preparation

Heat ghee in a pan.

Now add the amaranth flour and mix well. Roast the flour on low

flame for 5–7 minutes while stirring continuously. Cook till it is light brown and lets off a nutty fragrance.

In a medium-sized vessel, heat water and milk on medium flame. Add saffron to it.

Now add the warm milk to the flour and stir well to avoid the formation of lumps.

Add jaggery and cardamom and mix well.

Once the jaggery melts, turn the flame to low, place a lid on the pan and cook for 5–7 minutes.

When you remove the lid, you will see that the ghee has started to separate from the halwa. This means the halwa is ready.

Take 1 tbsp ghee in another pan and fry the walnuts and raisins. Keep aside.

In the pan with the leftover ghee, add apples and sugar.

Cook on high flame and let the apples caramelize.

Make quenelles or demould the sheera and then top it with ghee roast apples and nuts.

"*Packed with nutrients, gluten-free and comforting, this dish can also be made with bananas.***"**

Aditi Handa's

Sukhdi

🌿 KID-FRIENDLY

This jaggery-flavoured ghee bomb has nutritionist Aditi Handa's stamp of approval, so you don't need to feel guilty for indulging your sweet tooth.

Ingredients

1 cup whole wheat flour

¾ cup ghee

150 g jaggery

Preparation

Heat a pan on medium flame.

Add ¾ cup ghee.

Add atta to it and cook it until light brown.

You can add more ghee if you feel the mixture is too dense.

Once you start getting the sweet smell of halwa, you know it's almost ready.

Turn off the hob and add grated jaggery to it, incorporating it evenly.

While it's still hot, pour this into a flat container or thaali not more than ¾ inch in height and cut into squares.

Wait for an hour for it to cool and serve.

❝*Sukhdi is a Gujarati dish which can be eaten as a snack between meals or packed into kids' tiffins. It's very nutritious, so I keep it in my bag when I'm travelling.* ❞

Sucheta Sehgal's

Black Forest Pudding

Inspired by the classic black forest cake, this eggless, no-bake pudding by home chef Sucheta Sehgal, layered with whipped cream, chocolate, cherries and cashews, is the cheat dessert of your dreams.

Ingredients

6–8 slices white bread

6–8 tsp drinking chocolate powder

6–8 tsp demerara sugar

1 can cherries

½ cup chopped cashew nuts

2 cups fresh cream

4 tbsp grated chocolate

Preparation

Cut the bread slices into four pieces each and dry-blend in a mixer to make crumbs.

Add demerara sugar and drinking chocolate powder to this and mix well.

For the cream

Add sugar as per taste and whip well.

Deseed the cherries, keeping a few aside for topping.

To assemble the pudding

Take a glass bowl or glasses.

Put the chocolate–bread mix first.

Top it with cherries and cashews.

Then add whipped cream and repeat these layers till the bowl/glass is full and you get cream on top.

Sprinkle some grated chocolate and decorate with cream and cherries.

Chill and serve cold.

❝This 7-ingredient black forest pudding is perfect for when your kids are whining for home-made dessert but you don't want to put in too much effort, and it's also great for impromptu gatherings. ❞

Acknowledgements

What's in Your Dabba would not have been possible without a long list of people who were instrumental in putting this book together.

Food writer and journalist Vernika Awal who tested each recipe numerous times, painstakingly recreated the dishes and is responsible for all the delightful food imagery.

Tavishi Sahu who designed this book with a freshness and effervescence that perfectly embodies its spirit.

Copy editor Cincy Jose who displayed meticulous attention to detail.

The Tweak India team, especially Chandni Sehgal and Rochelle Pinto, who took on the mammoth task of bringing this book to fruition.

Twinkle Khanna who oversaw and gave her guidance on every aspect of this book – from the photoshoots to how the recipes would be written.

Publisher Chiki Sarkar who refused to contribute any recipes and only provided deadlines, but this book would not have been possible without her experienced guidance and her whip.

The entire team of Juggernaut Books who extended all their support.

All our contributors who gave us their wonderful recipes, their time and their unmatched enthusiasm.

List of contributors

List of dishes

Snack dabba

Cheat dabba

Index

A Note on Tweak India

Founded by Twinkle Khanna, Tweak India is a digital media company for modern multitaskers. A space for Indian women to challenge old ideas and discover new ones. Where nothing is sacred, except laughter.

juggernaut

THE APP FOR INDIAN READERS

Fresh, original books tailored for mobile and for India. Starting at ₹10.

juggernaut.in

1

CRAFTED
FOR MOBILE
READING

*Thought you would never read a book
on mobile? Let us prove you wrong.*

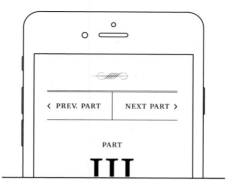

Beautiful Typography

The quality of print transferred
to your mobile. Forget ugly PDFs.

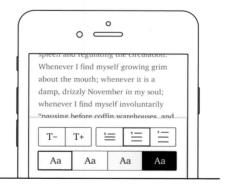

Customizable Reading

Read in the font size, spacing
and background of your liking.

AN EXTENSIVE LIBRARY

Including fresh, new, original Juggernaut books from the likes of Sunny Leone, Praveen Swami, Husain Haqqani, Umera Ahmed, Rujuta Diwekar and lots more. Plus, books from partner publishers and loads of free classics. Whichever genre you like, there's a book waiting for you.

DON'T JUST READ; INTERACT

We're changing the reading experience from passive to active.

Ask authors questions

Get all your answers from the horse's mouth.
Juggernaut authors actually reply to every
question they can.

Rate and review

Let everyone know of your favourite reads or
critique the finer points of a book – you will be
heard in a community of like-minded readers.

Gift books to friends

For a book-lover, there's no nicer gift than
a book personally picked. You can even
do it anonymously if you like.

Enjoy new book formats

Discover serials released in parts over
time, picture books including comics,
and story-bundles at discounted rates.
And coming soon, audiobooks.

LOWEST PRICES & ONE-TAP BUYING

Books start at ₹10 with regular discounts and free previews.